RITUALS OF LIGHT

© Wilga Rose 2001
This book is copyright. Apart from any fair dealing for the purposes of study and research, criticism, review, or as otherwise permitted under the Copyright Act, no part may be reproduced by any process without written permission. Inquiries should be made to the publisher.

Published by
Five Islands Press Associates,
PO Box U34
Wollongong University 2500
FAX 02 4272 7392
email kpretty@uow.edu.au

Acknowledgements
Poems in this book have been published in literary magazines including *Southerly, Quadrant, Poetry Australia, Meanjin, LiNQ, The Weekend Australian, The Paterson Literary Review* (US) and *Bogg* (US and UK) as well as the anthology *Up From Below* and the ABC radio program *A First Hearing*.

Cover design by Rachael Day
Original artwork by Orel Lea

National Library of Australia
Cataloguing-in-Publication Entry
Rose, Wilga, 1943
    Rituals of Light
    ISBN 0 86418 704 1
    1. Title
A821.3

Australia Council for the Arts

This project has been assisted by the Commonwealth Government through the Literature Fund of the Australia Council, the Federal Government's arts funding and advisory body.

RITUALS OF LIGHT

Wilga Rose

Five Islands Press

For Harvey and my family,
with love.

I would also like to acknowledge
and thank Varuna Writers' Centre,
and particularly Peter Bishop,
for help and support in writing
many of these poems

Contents

Last Seen	9
Black Swan to Currawong	10
Ferry Passing	11
Under Stars Canowindra	12
Clinical Psychology	13
First Photo	14
Sea Song	15
Fire	16
Looking at the Stars	17
Ferry Crossing	18
Isle of Iona	19
The Book of Kells	20
Fisherman, Bangally Head	21
The Collector	22
St Peter's, Surry Hills	23
Reflections	24
Senses	25
Moveable Feast	26
One Sunday Afternoon	27
Trial at Tribulation	28
Winter Beach	29
Heirlooms	30
Waverley Cemetery, Sunday Morning	31
Summer Dawn	32
Tai Chi	33
Surfer	34
Tracks	35
On the Escarpment	36
Timeless	37
Curtain Call	38

Small Expectations	39
Weather Man	40
Crucible	41
Fire Images	42
Unedited	43
Parakeet Café Katoomba	44
Main Street, Katoomba	45
Queen Victoria Lookout	46
In Eleanor Dark's Room	47
Mirror Images	48
Gateway	49
Travelling Light	50
Backward Up the Slopes of Sunny Air	51
Girl at a Bus Stop	52
Beyond Fences	53
Camera Shutter	55
Prisoner	56
Dead Leaves	57
Evening	58
Storm Silences	59
Still Life	60
Japanese Gardens Near Cowra	61
Rorchach	63
Spring Light with Flowers	64
Going Nowhere	66
At Mackerel Beach	67
Bondi Odyssey	68
I Ching	70
Medieval Herb Garden	71
Sculpture	72
Pilgrims	73

Rituals of Light

Last Seen

In the gardens at Vaucluse House
among the roses and camellias
and the dead voice of mauve hydrangeas,
we walked,
on Anzac Day, seeking a peace
among fronds of fern
and old world silences.
Suddenly around a bend,
a wheelchair granny,
in motorized glee,
accelerated,
and we were almost swept
to silence.
"Take it easy, mum,"
her daughter yelled,
as she churned up leaves
and stunned the dust and shadows.
She smiled.
Last seen among the marigolds,
brake off,
head high,
accelerating towards the sunset.

Black Swan To Currawong

Outside my window
walks a currawong
along the wires;
tightrope walking
between the cliff and sea.
A thing I could not dare
to do
with sanity
between my toes
and featherless
as Socrates.
And yet the other day
a black swan
in an ecstasy of swinging
blacked out whole suburbs;
forcing them
to feel among his feathers
for the light.

Ferry Passing

I have bought an ice cream
on the wharf and watch the ferry
licking its way across the harbor,
slipping yachts like stitches.
It is October, after the growth
of spring rain,
and sun spills mercury on water.
The *North Head* sits at the wharf
waiting a few minutes to departure,
then wades out towards the Heads,
sea opening to the scalpel of its bow,
digging deep to the ocean swell.
An old ferry, now
it's all wood and groans
rattling across water.
New ferries glide past
skimming surfaces,
dragonflies, hardly there.
The hydrofoil like thought
is in the future,
before the present takes breath;
the slow sway of the deck,
shudder of age
in its piston heart,
it's only a short distance now
in the shimmer of its wake;
the years passing.

Under Stars, Canowindra

Under a country sky
that flies crow's wing
slowly into night,
we lie, looking into galaxies,
there and not there,
watching time recede
in spinnakers of stars.
The night is bridal,
a veil falls down the sky.
Stars stare clear through the air,
the wand of Prospero,
conjuring destinies.
We cling with our backs
to this little planet,
looking upwards
where all the busy littleness
of living
flows downhill like rain
in a puddle,
light years away.

Clinical Psychology

Each morning, yet again,
the clinical psychology
of housework;
ordering the chaos,
the dirty clothes discarded
in dank piles,
the wild anarchy of breakfast,
children, half-dressed,
coming, going
showered, packed, shouting
and ready for the day.
On the radio the traffic's had
another nervous breakdown,
someone's murdered, deposed,
overdosed;
little happiness exposed in a naked world.
Scrubbing the bath and vacuuming
the floors,
I'm simply ordering the chaos;
a jacaranda blazes purple voices,
over the back fence the ritual swirl
of brooms in ten thousand houses
sings against the sea,
dust, dust
and dust again.

First Photo

    (To Eleanor, looking at her first photo, an ultrasound)

You look at yourself as you were
inside me,
a shadowed image
curled in reverie,
and smile.
Diving deep into the image
you can almost see
an arm,
a head, a swimming leg,
almost, not quite
it takes imagination to see
the bud erupt into
the flower.
Sleeping in a swag of water
you swung through
heart beat's pendulum,
opening slowly to the light,
you smile to see the moment
swinging
in that first unremembered sea.

Sea Song
(For Eleanor)

Suddenly like conscience
she kicks me,
thought and punctuation of feet
reminding me I'm not alone;
this other person in me
which is and isn't me,
the swag of flesh,
the brief darkness,
anonymity;
heartbeat thundering,
world a swimming capsule
of peace, tranquillity.
When I swim in the surf
each morning near dawn,
we sway together
in the same amniotic sac.

Fire
    (for Rohan)

The fire now is middle-aged,
the first crackles, leaps
and spurts have subsided.
A blue flame dances, iris flowers,
the logs are orange heat
expanding out into the room.
Grey shadows in it flicker,
fall to ash —
Ash — the ultimate dimunition.
Remembering the day
I took your ashes
in my lap,
to take you home,
and finally to the sea
at Dobroyd.
It was your mortal shell
but not your laugh
or spirit,
that, like fire,
glows on.

Looking At the Stars
(for Rohan)

It has been two years now,
since you left us,
the cold encyclical of death
running through you,
the horrible quiet of it all.
Somehow we struggled through long corridors
of pain, congealed silences
and the angry hunger for
lost moments,
the future unrealised,
the bread unleavened.
Where do I put your kindness and your laughter,
the sporting trophies
that glitter on the shelves?
Everywhere my eyes fish
your memory.
The photographs of you
in happy times with your girlfriend,
or at Dobroyd with a shark.
Yesterday I picked up a cigarette butt
outside your room,
"Don't smoke", I always said.
It didn't matter finally...
When you were little you would say
"Dad, can I look at the stars with you".
Tonight there are no stars,
only a grey cloak of cloud.
Yet somewhere, out beyond,
I know you are there,
with God, looking at the stars.

Ferry Crossing
   (for Rohan)

The lights are glowing,
constellations on suburban shores.
As night drifts in
across the harbour,
a quiet settles,
the ferry furrows water
as the jetcat skims
in panic
like a startled bird,
seeking safe havens.
Crossing the heads
the ferry rolls slowly,
wading through shadows.
Across the bay
I look to see lights
in the fisherman's huts
at Dobroyd,
but there are none.
It would have been his birthday soon,
at twenty four;
now he is with the sea,
the sandstone cliff,
and God,
beyond the canopy
of night
in another country.

The Isle of Iona

At the edge of the world, an island
flung like a stone, settled cold in a metallic sea.
Pilgrims, like Saint Columba in 563
who came to find peace under this distant ceramic blue
of sky,
we wandered the abbey's stone silences
and the wind wrapped round us in cold scarves
of light, shadowed by the ancient Celtic Cross.
In quiet cells of contemplation monks lit the world
with their illumination,
circle on circle, intricate as lichens,
of the jewel-cloaked Book of Kells, passed down
generations.
It holds the stillness like a candle on the altar,
haloed mystery spreading out
into the darkness.

The Book of Kells
(For Joel)

Brilliant,
the vivid etchings
of a labyrinth luminous
with swirls and echoes,
iridescent suburbs of the sea.
Design within design,
the structured estuaries of light
moving
to centres inland,
song within song,
island to island,
intricate as lichens.
Last night on television swayed
the frayed edges
of Ireland's Western coast,
the green bow of hills
sailing the soft blue spaces,
the open-mouthing sea
kissing the gravelled shore.
The donkey carts gnarl centuries,
plod on through poverty,
among dead caravans
on the edges of the town.
In Limerick, there was no rhyme
to work,
the bright land sagged
with the vivid burden of its youth
migrating, like lost birds
from the ragged fringes of poetry.

Fisherman, Bangalley Head
   (for Brendan)

A solitary fisherman stands
on a peninsula of rock,
casting out across the wave
into the open sea,
flat on its back
in a westerly's wintering thrust.
He stands beneath, willing the rod
to bend,
behind his shadow,
having baited the hook
at this small end of the world.
He knows his quarry
and time no longer barks
at his heels.
The earth spins on a slow axis,
spending the silence,
the parabola of rod,
willing it to bend
like horizons opening
to an infinity of fishes.
He waits there, silent
on a rock platform
beneath the suburbs.

The Collector
(for Brendan, Rohan and Joel)

As we go up the hill
together,
he runs ahead
to find the wealth
where stones
expire to air,
and seabirds wheel
and conjugate
the whips of light
beneath the surface
of the sea,
which might just be a meal.
Up the track's
old vertebraed back
we climb;
and as he goes
my son collects,
a mussel shell, three nuts
of different sizes, and pebbles
of purest marble;
they shine new-minted
in his treasury of eyes.
"Look at these", he says.
I glance briefly,
busy with my swag,
collecting bits of scarab-sea
and sky
and a child's eyes.

St. Peter's, Surry Hills
(For Harvey)

This church has an inner silence,
womb-like, waiting for footsteps
to cross thresholds,
enter,
pray,
or simply sit
watching candles
wavering to extinction,
breaking the bread of darkness.
Old migrant women come,
scarved and shuffling
in rituals of shadow,
moving among gold ghosts
of saints,
counting rosaries.
Amid the polished light
of stained glass certainties,
they are leaves of fire
waving in wind.

Reflections

Along the resonance
of light,
the lake holds still,
pelicans stand
solid,
studying survival.
The car is caught
in traffic,
and pants
like a trapped animal.
Quiet, the water
brims
with reflections,
tree, rock, time,
the cool meniscus
of discovery.
Still, as the centre
of the eye,
the earth,
for once,
spins slowly.

Senses

My senses close
like flowers without light,
shrink into themselves
behind the garden fence,
the repetition of the days
goes on,
paling and paling,
almost extinct
in its own lifetime.
Along the lake,
brimming
with autumn shadows,
leaves;
the detritus of summer
gone,
I see the pelican
move upward into air,
its huge wings
surfing sideways
on the wind
in parabolas of light,
and suddenly
I am awake.

Moveable Feast

A look out the window
and banksias sway
with morning wind.
Lorikeets drift in
jagged primaries of purple, green,
the sky stilettoed
with a hibernating maple gum,
linking with the dead masts
of the bay, asleep at moorings.
Downhill in brackets is the beach,
netted between headlands,
the sea somersaults,
spread skirts up sand,
lace silences;
the roar of sea in shells.
Across the hills
the shriek of cockatoos
shreds dawn like calico
white and drifting.
The mangrove swamp swims dimly
through primeval mud,
crab and lightning fishes flash
with one mind
through the shallows;
the sun, throwing rusty backdrop
in the west
goes down singing.

One Sunday Afternoon

Although it is 4.30,
I have a midnight feeling
of silence,
stillness,
wind bedded in the leaves,
clouds hauled in across the bay,
space curved, as Einstein knew it,
the air pock-marked
with light,
cut glass fractures upward
and is lost in brilliance.
I stop the hurried ministry
of housework,
dust my eyes,
silk on curved eyeball,
dilated flight
out into the street,
up trees, on shell-charged beaches,
the moment holds,
flutters,
exactly bridal
between reticence and passion.

Trial At Tribulation

And yet again,
fern, wild orchid, tree canopy,
tropical rainforest's lush imagery;
this wild green womb should never be
torn curtain against the sky.
Macrocosm, microcosm,
buttress of roots,
leaf, vine and flower
exist
and then resume
their fertile legacy to all
the multitudinous life
that crawls and creeps and hops
beneath.
Planetary lungs heave
for more trees,
and still bulldozers come
to flatten and distress wildom,
wash heirlooms into earth
with roads through rainforests;
rain without forest,
myopic strategies allow
the random element
of weeds and power
to colonise, destroy
this last kingdom of trees;
on trial
at Tribulation.

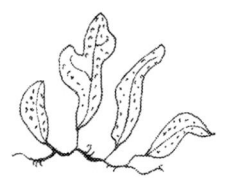

Winter Beach

After the rain
the beach has a flat mythology
Sponge, seaweed, driftwood,
in an agony of shapes,
tide-sculptured.
Breakers in relentless
cavalry,
surge shoreward, wind plumed.
Winter's grey silence is unhinged.
A dog barks down his fences.
Old gods drag
at my feet,
the tide is moving
out,
sea invades me,
shears off my head
with a wreath of foam,
I feel the old ice
glitter in my bones.

Heirlooms

On a ridge nearby the chain saw shrieks
the fall of trees,
executed.
Bird, fern, flower,
suddenly evicted
to the open sky.
Here is the other autumn,
a fall of shredded chips.
Behind, a storm is gathering,
bruised hills.
Rain forest is nothing now
but rain.
It withers wet sobs
to wrinkled premature senility;
the fossil heirloom ferns
washed into drawers of earth.

Waverley Cemetery, Sunday Morning

Morning sun's clear light
on old tombs
in Waverley cemetery.
They roll down to the sea,
the polished marble crosses,
angels and the vases
full of flowers.
Here it's full house
with the man killed by a coach
in 1880, and the child who lies
beneath iced marble,
and a man,
born in Ireland,
greening the fringes of poetry.
I stand beside Kendall,
Lawson and Mackellar
growing towards sky,
their swag of words
sings down
the sea.
Across the cliff
a pale shroud
on a coathanger of sun.

Summer Dawn

How often have I come here
to this beach;
its old familiar features glance at me
hardly noticing.
Suddenly dawn light on sandstone cliffs
brightly burrowing,
gradations of yellow shadow.
I'll sit here on the sand
and stare out to the silver rim
of seeing,
the shell-encrusted shore,
the open territories of sky,
thinking of cages, bars
and the structures of each day;
whose word is silence.

Tai Chi

On crippled sand
cold under slow light,
a dancer comes,
before dawn shadows
are hauled in by a net of light.
She slowly lifts and drifts an arm
across the wave
moving with cloud's grace,
effortlessly.
A trance of silence,
then slow shift of movement,
like trees submitting to the wind.
Among dune shadows she is dim-lit,
weaving together earth and sea.
Slowly, with one hand,
she conjures up
the sun.

Surfer

You see him skiing down the heat of summer,
along the wave that takes him nowhere;
sometimes he sits, quiet as cormorants
studying seasons,
retracing watery moments
one by one,
the calm horizon,
the nettled sun,
waiting his chance;
the perfect curve and flow
of the wave
that never comes.
Out beyond the rim
of land
a mesh of water
binds him.

Tracks

A beach,
wind-scoured,
featuring built-in obsolescence
of white light falling
in long feathers across a creeping surf.
Shallow to shallow it curls
on the sandbank
neat and prim,
lace petticoats drifting.
Sand; no prints
which would shadow human sabotage,
white flakes of seagulls reed-thin,
spin the wind.
On runways of white sand
they have left their signatures,
clear, three-pronged arrows pointing
across the dunes
to sky.

On the Escarpment

Walking through tree ferns
arms of ghost gums,
rags of bark
and the rush of water over rock,
falling, falling.
The path heads down
into the valley swathed in clouds.
A currawong calls.
There are no signposts here,
the path leads somewhere,
the only way to know
is to keep on walking.
Trees are mentors and keep
close counsel,
mosquitoes rise from a dance
of a thousand summers.
The old rocks lean on the sky.
The path leads on
but there are choices,
walking, taking chances,
there are always changes,
and you can't go back.

Timeless

Through an arch of rock
I walked.
Kicking off shoes and mud
and sat silent,
on the edge of sandstone skirts
flung out into the valley.
Above it all
the mist, rolling in clouds
across huddled trees.
Calm, apart from water
swirling,
abseiling down chasms,
a bird, celebrating morning,
just me and God
chatting quietly
over a cup of silence;
and then a bouncing couple,
dread-locked and worn
by green enthusiasm
with whirring cameras
and munching shoes,
said,
'What's the time?'
and I didn't know.

Curtain Call

The view is blank
as a computer screen,
white curtains drawn
to preserve essential privacy
of the valley and the cliffs,
an irrelevance of people.
Nearby a ghost gum
does a strip-tease,
swinging tattered clothes
in sky-light breezes
drifting in.
Backpackers have nothing
to photograph,
only the white innocence
of unwritten air,
the call of birds,
echo of voices
and the insistent mantra
of live water,
falling.

Small Expectations

Somehow I always manage
to wear the wrong clothes
for the occasion,
as tramping around the edge
of the escarpment
the precipice of air
are walking people
in thick boots, strong denims, rain
jackets, daypacks and serious
faces,
as if fault lines
in their geography
had frozen.
On a strange planet
nearby are those who wear
ballgowns at bus stops
barefeet in mud puddles
ankle satin-soft,
and in my black velvet pants,
and suede shoes
among tree ferns and sassafras,
I dance a minuet.

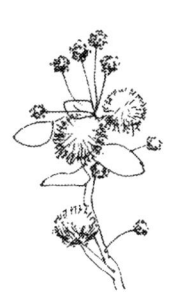

Weather Man

Just now the sun slipped out
for a stroll, after days of mist
and rain.
I ran to sit in a pool of it,
wallow in the warmth,
watch the bright azaleas glisten.
Then, offended, it withdrew
like an insulted lover,
with a cool grey bow as it departed.
Should I go out now
prepared for all weathers,
leather-coated, umbrellaed, strong-shoed,
or like mad Lear
on the verge of whether
throw off clothes, pretences,
drown the banalities of skin and bone,
or be civilised and correct
as the TV weatherman.

Crucible

In an upstairs room
at Varuna,
a plaintiff moth
swings by a gallows rope
of silken thread,
spinning and spinning
at the end of its tether
in a last valiant
assertion of vitality.
The ministering spider
plays its doom,
slowing the last vestiges
of life
to black futility.
Delicate spindles
of a living death,
poised between sky
and earth
in aching vulnerability.
Slowly I put out my hand
to set it free,
but glass windows come
between.
Seeing, like God, the suffering
and savagery and knowing,
pain must be a crucible
for life.

Fire Images

There is something essentially
beautiful
in an open fire;
logs leaping light
and shuffling to ash,
domesticated in the grate
eating wood like greedy carnivores.
I love to watch the hours
breaking in Dante's inferno,
shifting strata, deeper,
untouchable,
images transmogrifying.
In childhood, curled in an antique
chair,
watching smoke ascending
and the changing pattern
of the coals;
alone, late at night
in ancient comfort,
and in the morning
cleaning the grate and tiles
was a happy penance.

Unedited

The bees are hunting nectar
in wisteria fronds;
it leans on the wall,
an old arthritic lady,
veteran of many springs.
Below are bright serrated leaves
of strawberries
and little knobs of fruit,
tarot of summer.
A hanging basket swings
empty bounty from a branch
and swords of green
are fencing in the air.
Some empty terracotta pots
half-filled with litter,
a birds-nest fern,
and the odd daffodil,
grow where they will,
nothing crossed out,
a fuse of wild energy.
And next to me
a washing basket
catches the rain.

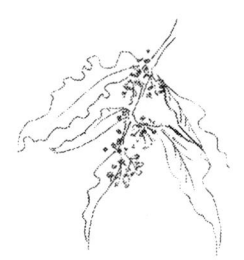

Parakeet Cafe, Katoomba

The young girl opposite,
with bracelets, earrings, nose-ring,
everything,
sips her tea with studied nonchalance,
and then a smile, a laugh
as he comes in,
The one she has been waiting for.
He has acne, reticence and a pack
of cigarettes she takes,
assuredly.
Her fifteen summers shine
solar and certain,
"How did you know it was me?"
she says,
the answer drowns in tea.
He grabs her hand,
she reaches for the sugar, smiling.
Suddenly she's gone,
her shoulder-bag patiently waiting.
Then another couple join them,
the smoke curls
into ancient laughter,
circling possibilities……

Main Street, Katoomba

It's uphill all the way
with three small kids
and a second-hand stroller,
her cigarette burns like a talisman
of doom.
The old couple, hardly noticing each other,
shuffle sideways,
he, in his red cap, a plastic rain-coat,
has seen it all.
She is not so sure and talks
to telegraph poles, too rude to answer.
Next to the antique shop
a bearded busker assembles his flute and waits,
backpackers stagger onwards
the weight of the unseen world
on their backs.
On street seats, old people sit
and stare at yesterdays.
A group of artists smile and hug
each other.
Outside the fish shop a woman says;
"I had a dream...two years ago....",
as if it mattered.

Queen Victoria Lookout

I have gone out early
barefoot,
to walk down the cliff
to rainforest,
the mud is satin squelches underfoot,
the roar of water
fills the unedited air.
The valley, a sea of opaque white
surfing the sandstone edges.
Clear sky, no people anywhere,
currawongs sing casually in gums,
deep down the valley's mystery
is safe,
its ancient heart beating,
long after I
am gone.

In Eleanor Dark's Room
(at Varuna)

Old sepia photographs of a boy, laughing,
and a sombre one,
in hand-knitted jumper,
have not faded.
They are the legacy of flesh and blood
she left us, the books and memories.
On the door jamb, with a mother's care,
she marked every inch
of the way,
2 years six months, three years nine months
5 years six months....
until at last, full grown
at 24 years 9 months
the saga stops.
Now there are other things
to count, with a mother's care;
her grandchildren
climb the door.
The room has a happy ambience
of growth and love
and words which bind us
to each other.

Mirror Images

Catching myself in a net
of eyes.
I notice my mother
looking back at me,
colours are different
but the shapes the same,
the sinuous romanticism
glowing.
Just when you think you're unique,
a special flower
in a diverse garden,
you see
the eyes, the image of another
glancing through you

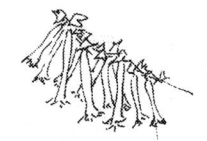

Gateway

The gateway to the garden
mauves with wisteria,
crab-apple soft-petalling,
keeping time with the seasons.
Yesterday, I saw a black cat
flouncing past, ears back,
out of his territory,
in a hurry.
When I called out,
he paused, scowled,
took out his pocket watch
then vanished behind
a bright azalea bush.
Unlike Alice,
I didn't follow.

Travelling Light

Travelling light
with only my eyes for luggage,
I turn the pages of the glossy magazine,
with Renoir's dancing couple
on the cover.
I'm flying to St. Paul's, Cornwall
and Stonehenge,
onto lakes and castles,
towers and swans
and green shadows on hills
under Ben Bulben,
sailing her prow seaward
to Atlantic ravages
of wind and wild rain,
log fires in a pub
and songs that sing
over and over.
I look and smile, transported instantly
from hammered sun
and beaches,
to wild mists, thatched cottages
and donkey carts
that bump along the cheap road
of my imagination.

Backward Up the Slopes of Sunny Air

I am leaning over fences
gazing into blue futures
— the hypothesis of hope.
When I am older,
I say,
I'll wear long dresses and a cape
and carry a basket
with a chameleon in it.
I'll jangle gold jewellery
and travel
like a gypsy on trains,
forgetting destinations
and ending up
at Moree,
west of the sunset.
On the street, I'll mumble
derelict verses
and muster abandoned ideas, like cars
in vacant lots,
that have no connections.
In the evening I'll sit
with a glass of Mateus and a cat
and wander backwards
up the slopes of sunny air
to my youth, then
go forth picking frangipani
and hydrangeas
over fences.

Girl at a Bus Stop

A barefoot girl in a yellow dress
at a bus stop,
eating a carrot,
is sky and stars,
beaches of yellow sand,
the long line of the land around her,
streets, avenues of maples
gums, the fine clipped grass,
immaculate houses,
pointed poplar fingers;
she spreads herself carelessly
over suburban asphalt,
cars stopped at lights
haul anchors of mortgages,
rusting;
lusting,
she bites a chunk of carrot
thinks of journeys,
destinations,
before she settles solid
in dead pastures,
years on.

Beyond Fences
    (for Bee Miles)

Living free, she'd call it,
beyond fences,
with an allowance that sheltered her from want,
she'd set out on a jaunt to Brisie
or Thursday Island,
"to cavort and do the stomach dance".
Jumping a rattler in the thirties
the driver let her drive
a few miles,
"I wished the fireman and engine driver
would disappear, and leave me to
the wind and trees".
In Cairns it was hot, but
"I jumped like a jaguar
at a miner's offer to see his mine".
There I walked with Aborigines
and George Watkins —
it was the children I loved,
black-eyed and barefoot.
We pretended we were legionnaires
scanning a far horizon for adventure.
Always on the move, camping out,
reciting Shakespeare for two shillings
— though I didn't need it.
Hardly noticed the Depression,
with its shabby sadness of fretted lives,
I slept in the stormwater drain
at Rushcutter's Bay,
with the derros and drunks.
Always a taxi nearby
to terrorise, though I always paid
my way.
In the end, I was fat, sloppy, rather
tattered in an old great coat

and green eyeshade for company,
when the Church took me in.
But, I'd sailed like a galleon
in a sea of skiffs,
heading out into unknown waters,
slowly, deliberately
with defiant courage,
beyond a land of picket fences...
living free."

Camera Shutter

Morning. Click.
Sunswung into iced sky.
Screech of parrots.
An overload of words on radio,
tow trucks drag off the wreckage,
a trailer, unconscious
on the harbour bridge.
Still life. Click.
Derelicts under bridges
at the quay,
dreaming dawn through flagons,
and the grapes gone sour
in a happy sleep.
Conjunction of planets,
desert sands burning,
driftwood on the beach.
Click.
Tide turning.
Burning sand to glass,
last fishes
flying across the face of sun,
loaves and flying fishes
enough for everyone.
Click.
You can hear guns growling
in sleep,
arsenals of fear,
news headlines shudder
in all directions,
Rorschach flowers,
the world is turning
on a hair trigger,
Click.

Prisoner

In a glass jar
in a bedroom,
sits a butterfly
fished from the sky's
summer light,
held captive by a rope of glass
it watches us move round
in endless freedom.
Spreading blue triangles
on accents of night,
it dreams of garden's
magic greenery.
In nervous flight
it twitches briefly,
then subsides
to mere philosophy of waiting.
At last its martyred silence
was too much,
we set it free
into the blue-winged emptiness
of sky.
It fluttered haltingly.
Yesterday I thought I saw it,
still within the garden fence of trees
keeping inside the well-flown territories,
against the vast explosion
of the sky.

Dead Leaves

I have become a miser
with words,
collecting them in ancient nooks,
dusting them off,
presenting them as valuable antiques
to the uninitiated;
phantasmagoria,
divers halcyon days,
athwart a pullulating bower,
diurnal fornications.
Silently they creep around
scattering themselves
like dead leaves
in forgotten alleys
of verse,
somehow new, yet withered by disuse,
they are raked into ritual piles,
to be sorted, aborted,
recycled in the growing compost
of decaying meaning.

Evening

Noose of light, growing thinner
round the neck of evening.
A broken window,
the shouts and shrieks of children,
wind shuffling among gums,
a dying deck of cards.
Grasping the moment
I move into shadow,
down the road to the beach,
where only a dog and two surfers
hollow water.
The dunes hold dark breasts
against the sky,
horizon of corrugated water,
as I slip under evening shadow,
beneath the wave,
wash away the dust,
the day,
in a baptism of water.

Storm Silences

I should have know when the wild storm
blew in from the west
flaying washing, scouring silences
as the sheep huddled under gums,
that your words were cut glass
ready to shatter any moment,
pursed lips that rankled
murdering years of friendship
in a few sharpened words
that scarred the air deliberately
it seemed,
putting a swathe of words
between us
a volcanic flow
of bitterness flowing downhill
into night.
You may as well have hit me,
I was stunned,
the silly littleness of it all.
Outside, the stars, light years away
lit ancient fossils in the riverbed.

Still Life

Early morning, with mist
crouching over hills
like prayer,
sheep startle as I walk
slowly up the winding red road
to the old house,
It stands now, derelict
its gum tree posts support verandahs
overlooking paddocks
where sheep stand apprehensive,
chewing silently.
Ropes of wisteria tangle and explode
in purple candelabra dripping next to bougainvillea.
A spider hangs on a trapeze of light
between the orange and the lemon trees,
heavy with summer fruit.
Thistles charge the air
and grasses glitter
after the night's wild rain.
As I walk among the oranges and nectarines,
eating slowly,
last night's lava flow of words and silences
subsides to ash,
years cremated suddenly,
as trivial as the summer storm
that flashed, departed.
And yet, the old house is painted
in my mind,
still life;
I know I will not see this place
again.

Japanese Gardens
    (Near Cowra)

We had come to the gardens
from dry plains,
the dead hair of grasses,
drifting hot winds,
away from the kid's incessant banter
to the netted tranquillity
of a garden,
carefully plotted, planted, flowered.
Immaculate waterfalls
over marble pebbles
and long hair of weed
drifting over ledges, carelessly.
A path wound round
amongst painted vivids of petunias
purple and pink,
the sculptured rocks
so carefully positioned
haiku to haiku;
the meditative pool,
rock to polished rock,
the sky blue-washed
against primary greenery.
Then we rested in the Tea House
at the top;
the wide pool's stone lantern,
below the quiet cell of water
ceramic colours of the flowers
fired under a glaze of sun.
Beyond the inner centre of still thought,
a feeding jetty
where the carp savaged water
with piranha frenzy.
And out beyond the bracketed gates,
the small ascendancy of human order,

wild nudity of sky,
gums clutching red clay silences,
brown tussocks of drained grasses,
and behind mauve hills,
the organic wilderness
of the plains.

Rorschach

It's all in the brain
he said,
like a Rorschach inkblot
going nowhere,
yet everywhere
and many things fly from its inky depths;
butterflies with spider's faces
a castle with a pair of eyes
an old and wind demented tree....
making some sense
from that ink takes a few moons,
my friend,
sense distilled from chaos
is always a tricky operation.
The days flowed on
and still the blot refused to speak.
Perhaps it's quite forgotten
who it is, they said,
(ink of amnesia?)
"It's all in the brain," he said.
"Nothing objective,
but you must see what is there".

Spring Light With Flowers

We walked along the beach
to where the light's radiance
was blue opal,
setting against the rock face
which we climbed;
up the fire trail
on a September day,
buzzing with wildflowers,
pink boronia and native rose.
Spider flowers in grey and red,
budding green flannel flowers
red native fuschia's tiny bells,
clutching the web of sky,
the air burning colour like fuel
to light the way of Spring.
Up on the high plateau,
dazzling above the sea
wrens and honeyeaters fly
among heath, red, white and pink,
white cockatoos shriek
tearing down sky.
Here too, fringed lily, wild orchids
ferns curling their hair amongst rocks,
a marvellous moment
of purple, white, green
dredged up from rock;
banksias burning torches among gums,
flowering white, exploding fireworks
of feathered flight.
All this in arid country,
colour-textured with a dry brush,
light sweeps like a gong
inside your head,
the ancient power of earth resisting
and on a high rock plateau

above the sea,
Aboriginal carvings of men,
turtles, fish,
forty thousand years turning stars dark;
the curved signature of people
who lived in harmony with
rock, gum tree, flannel flower,
the wave's eternal power
flowing tidal through memory;
dinosaur, country
time and carving
of a continent's remembering

Going Nowhere

I have boarded a ferry,
headed for the zoo,
although I don't expect to see
any animals.
Going nowhere - heading out
undirected,
dropping time like stitches,
below the wide arc of the bridge
and grey sails of winter sky.
The ferry churns wide furrows in the water,
it is simply passing time
slowly moving
towards a question mark,
the jetty at the far end
of the harbour.
The view is a paradox of bush
and wild units
clutching the foreshore.
Everything in its place,
the ferry pulls out
across the water
rolling in a soft cradle.
The afternoon is stretching
light,
across its bow,
fallow shadows fall.
Going nowhere at no particular
time, without speed,
the ultimate luxury
of all.

At Mackerel Beach

A bright clear winter's day;
doing the round trip on the ferry
to Mackerel Beach,
the wild bright silence
as it slips through
light-encrusted sky,
across the little bays and beaches,
The Basin, Currawong,
the permed hair of trees
growing from sandstone,
picnickers coming and going,
and campers with their backpacks,
off for just a nibble of the primitive;
firelight and bush silences,
strange rustlings and winds flapping
in the night.
At last we reach the jetty,
and make our way up the track
to a cluster of houses
snuggling up to the cliff
behind the beach,
among the palms, banana fronds
and rosellas screeching in the banksias.
Slowly we settle for the day,
away from routines and the clock.
The sun washes up thoughts,
driftwood at the edge of sand,
as we sit on the beach
watching the slow ferries drift by.

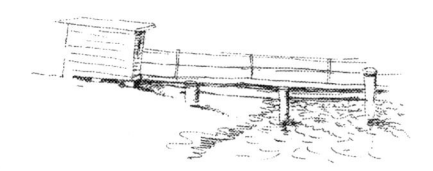

Bondi Odyssey

I have caught three buses
and a ferry
to get here,
where I began
the long wide arc of sand
clear-cut under white winter light.
Above the beach a huge red kite
skiis slopes of sunny air,
dipping and weaving.
Unravelling fresh-cooked chips
and calamari
in the park beside the beach
I'm accosted by a mafia
of seagulls squawking obscenities
at me,
as fish smells drift on the wind.
Along the promenade,
everything's the same,
the long waves rolling in
lipped with foam,
the pavilion, the surfclub,
even the children's pool
with the tide — swirling in,
remembers me.
It could be 1963.
A solitary surfer
in a wetsuit
paddles like cormorants
against the surge of
wave on wave,
throwing up white hair
into the wind.

And buses cruise
endlessly familiar tracks

unchanged in generations,
as Japanese tourists run from waves,
chasing them up the shoreline.

Around the shopping area
wind scours surfaces
lifts paper into careless
scattered heaps,
among the frayed and fretting
buildings,
liver-red brick and peels of paint.
The skyline is unchanged,
as dense as beehives
stack on stack,
the narrow canyons of the streets
arrayed with cars.
Years have darkened them,
the trees join hands
over narrow roads.
All shops have metamorphosed,
except the fruit market,
Bate's milkbar and Stark's Kosher Deli,
immovable in generations.
Houses lie empty
with warnings on the door,
barring the silence.
In my old stone house
on the corner,
the only view is bars
across the window
threats of 'crime control'
on the door
and a stone lion
presiding over all.
The streets have seen a century come and go,
beyond the headland
a plane flies in
across the cliff-edge cemetery
crossing the skyline.

I Ching
("The Book of Changes")

In a glass jar,
near the pot plants,
eight tadpoles grope
in a veil of sand
dredged from a rock pool
nursery at Oxford Falls.
Move the jar,
and they twist and streak
like
giant sperm
across the treeless plain.
Nowhere to hide.
Not one thing
or the other;
their leggy ambiguity
leaps the boundaries of water.
They are survivors.

Medieval Herb Garden

The wormwood cuts the wind
with silver scissors,
and fronds of fern hang
on the fennel bush.
Here in the garden
where the peppermint cuts
with fresh essence
the high noon air.
And rosemary tries to remember,
what's his name?
Old comfrey heals the bones
and feeds the snails,
and borage stars
in mornings of bright blue.
The wind stirs up
a witch's medieval brew,
minus frog's legs, tadpoles,
eye of newt and rue!

Sculpture

Each day goes by
in light and darkness;
and chipping on you go,
at the soapstone
of your children,
carving with wind
and sea,
their thoughts words
armoury;
with television jingles
foremost in their brain.
How do you do it?
shouts the crowd,
bleating at the gateway
to the abattoir of dreams,
it's money,
all the way,
and yet you chip
hoping the chisel
engraves on their estuary
of blood
a home for unicorns.

Pilgrims
for Harvey

It's autumn and the coral trees spend leaves like wishes
in the last lilt of warmth
we are down the road now of a new century,
pilgrims on the road together,
travelling, unravelling the skeins of silence, word by word.
We're shuffling snapshots of the past: at a protest rally
or in Portugal on a cliff near Lourenco, in an abbey on Iona,
with the kids on a Manly ferry, hauling them from the outer deck
to safety, as we sculpted their moments one by one.
We are walking now, as pilgrims on the journey
in kaleidoscopic time,
always together for each other
and open to new mysteries beyond the bend in the road,
we just keep walking
towards the light.